EPITOME OF "ALMOSTS"

AND I 'ALMOST' SAID IT TO YOU

SHRUTI GAUTAM

Copyright © Shruti Gautam
All Rights Reserved.

To my heart, which I gave you.

Contents

Contents

Preface

They say you experience grief when you lose someone or something that hold so dear, even the thought of never being able to see them again makes your insides churn. I say that acquire grief when you can`t have someone you`ve been waiting your whole life for as well. Or even worse, they have someone they want so damn much that they would flip over the world for them and that, that someone isn't you, or worse still, it was never meant to be you. There are 5 stages of grief: DENIAL, ANGER, BARGAINING, DEPRESSION and ACCEPTANCE. The fifth stage is debatable. Accepting the loss is something which can never be attained if you ever were in love with them. Everytime you'd think of them, you'd be filled with bittersweet memories of the times when you had a hope for a-happily-ever-after.

Acknowledgements

This book could not have happened without the immense support of many of my very dear frinds, my brother and of course without the heart I apparently got broken. Images in the book belong to the respective owners and production companies.

Prologue

It's hard to wait around for something that I know isn't going to happen. But you know what's more difficult than that? Waiting around for it because it's everything that I'm ever going to need.

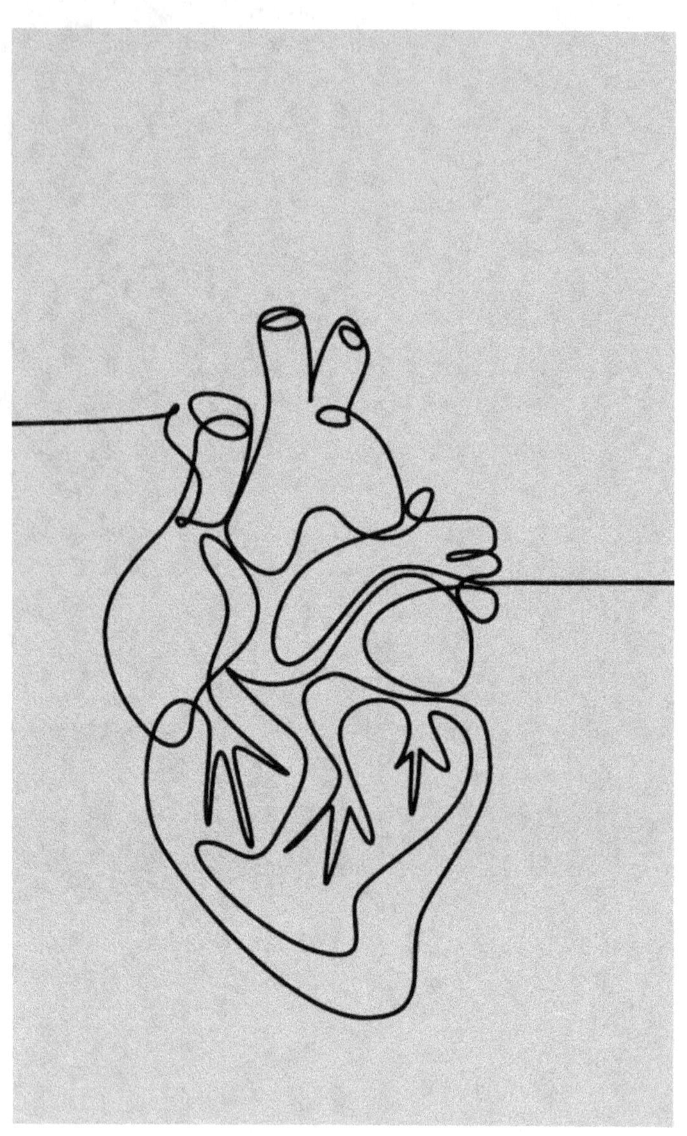

Stages Of Grief

STAGE I

Denial

~

STAGE II

Anger

~

STAGE III

Bargaining

~

STAGE IV

Depression

~

STAGE V

Acceptance

1. STAGE I

~~DENIAL~~

2. *

Do I Wanna Know?
Arctic Monkeys
Maybe I'm too
Busy being yours
To fall for somebody
new
Spotify

3. *

I've built a house,
In my head.
I call it, 'our house'
In case we'd never have one.
And there I've got everything,
Which I know we won't have.
I've got you dogs,
And a lot of plants,
Just as you like.
And I've got myself you,
Just as I'd like.
I've got ourselves a chance,
Which we'd never get to have.
I've got us a future,
And a present,
I've got us all the time,
In the world.
I've got us everything,
We won't get, in this life.
So, instead I've got,
It all in my head.

4. *

I am sick of being afraid to look you
in the eye, because I am going to fall for you,
land on my ass and break my heart, all over again.

~

Maybe I just loved the idea of you.
The idea, of a second heart.

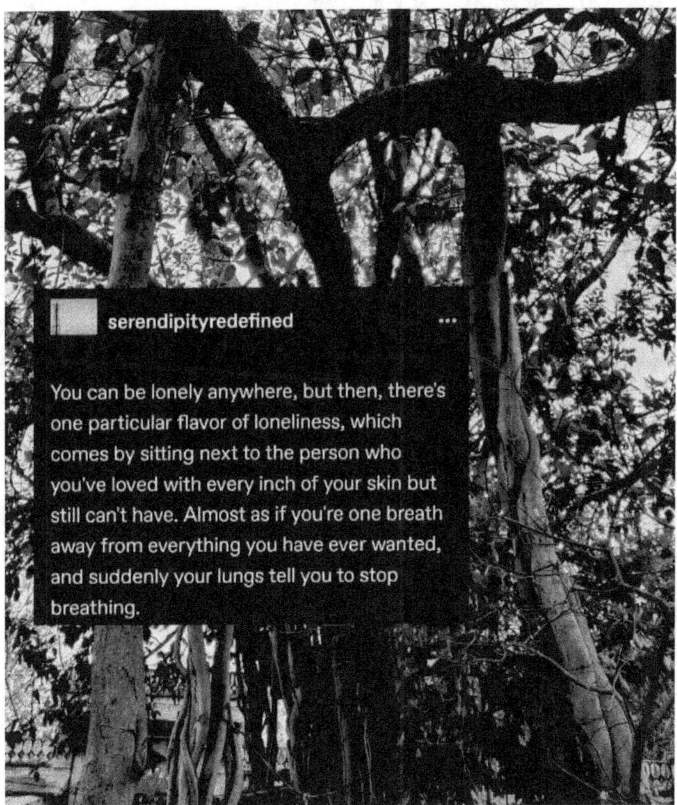

serendipityredefined

You can be lonely anywhere, but then, there's one particular flavor of loneliness, which comes by sitting next to the person who you've loved with every inch of your skin but still can't have. Almost as if you're one breath away from everything you have ever wanted, and suddenly your lungs tell you to stop breathing.

6. *

I know how terribly bad you are for me.
I'd give myself a hundred reasons to not be with you,
And then, you'd smile at me, and I'd forget them all at once.
Just like a moth, attracted to flame.
I'd burn away, go poof, if it means I get to be near you,
Even for a split-second.

It's nice , we didn't happen.

We'd have been too real for the world.

At least, this is what I tell myself.

7. STAGE II

~~ANGER~~

8. *

I Just Want to B...
Boxout
I don't want to set the world on fire
I just want to start
A flame in your heart
Spotify

9. *

I hold on to stuff, things, and more stuff. I cling to everything - I remember what was being said to me, what was said about me. I've kept the tinsy-tiny rose someone gave me almost two years ago - obviously wilted. I've restored the twig, my love was playing with some months ago.

I remember every word of the sentence that my mother blurted out when I was 5, which I didn't like. And I'm not proud, but I've got boxes under my bed overflowing with stuff that most people wouldn't keep. There's a reason why my closet is overflowing, I can't give up the old, tattered t-shirt because it reminds me of something, which I feel is important to remember.

And I didn't know that I don't let go, until one day. When my mom shouted at me,"YEAH, KEEP REMEMBERING ALL THAT HAPPENED. KEEP BURDENING YOURSELF WITH THE PAST. DON'T COME CRYING TO ME WHEN YOU REALIZE IT'S TOO LATE TO LET GO"
And I realized that I won't. Not to her anyways.

10. *

If I had known, that you'd fall for someone else, I'd have held you a little while longer in my arms. I'd have held your hand, for maybe a little second more. If I had known, that you wouldn't remember the last time we kissed, I'd have lingered a bit longer on your lips.

I'd have looked at you for a split second and a half more, took all of it in, if I had known it would be the last time. I would have had an extra giggle, while you smiled at the flirty little comments I passed.

I would have lit an extra cigarette that evening, if I had known that would be the last time, before I actually realized that it was never meant to be. Before I, actually, got it through my head that, we're the exact opposite of "meant-to-be".

I wouldn't have frowned at you for reeking of gin while you kissed me, if I had known it would be just in my head from now on. That no matter what I would do or have done for you, you're gonna be the the most heartbreaking "almost" that I had.

I would have asked you one more time, whether you loved me, if I had known I ain't gonna get the chance again. But maybe it was better that way. I didn't know if I had it in me to look at you while you deny it one more time.

I would have told myself one final lie, that maybe I could have you, before I knew it in my heart, it's never gonna happen. No matter what. If I had known that this love is gonna be such a waste, I would have loved you a little less.

......

11. *

I honestly wish ,
Ihad met you a long time ago.
You would have been
Long gone by now.

I wanted to be your
second favourite song.

12. *

You pleaded to me, one evening, to not judge you.
I asked, "Judge you for what?"

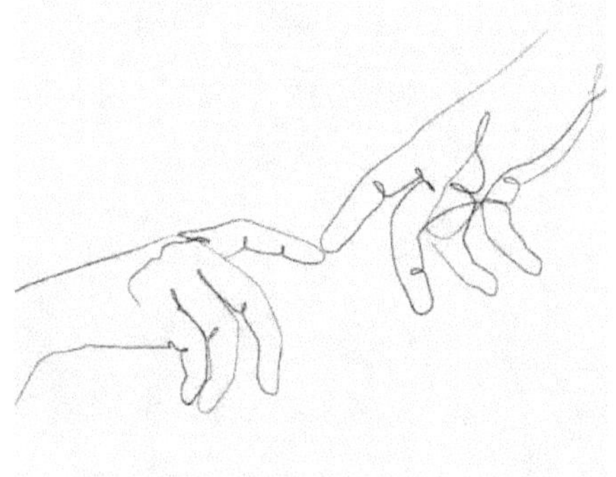

"For tonight."
"If I'd ever wanted to judge you, I already have a thousand
different reasons to do it.", I say.
"Why didn't you then?"
"Because probably I haven't loved someone so much before.
Or maybe because I don't know how to love someone like this
again." I tell you. You pull me into a hug.
"Please try not to ever leave me.",you say, drunkenly.
And I laugh.

***

Sad thing?

You didn't remember it the next morning.

13. STAGE III

~~BARGAINING~~

14. *

serendipityredefined

'Did you really love him that much?'

If you could ever, ever understand how
much I did, even you'd bawl out your eyes
when you see me, looking at him.

• 17 •

15. *

"Say it, say it, say that you love her dammit. You know, she does", my best friend goes on rambling, while being drunk, to you.
"Say that you love her."
"A lot", you tell her, knowing that I'm listening.
Yeah, sure. I believe you.
*

"I never had that type of feelings for you", you explain to me.
"Yeah, that's okay", I smile.
I can deal with that, I tell myself. But can I?
*

"There's no explanation. I was drunk. I don't have feelings for you. I'm sorry", you again explain to me.
"You expect me to buy this?"
"That's upto you, but that's the truth", you say.
I guess I'd just push it behind us. But should I?
*

"If you're really hurting because of me, I won't stop you", you ask me teary eyed.
"I am. You know I am"
"You can take as much time as you want. But come back again, okay?"

"I can't promise you that. You know that I can't. I won't make a promise, I can't keep"
"I don't want to let you go"
Then stop me. Make me stay. But both of us know that you won't. So let's just get this over with.
And I walk away. For real this time. And even if I stay, it won't be me.

16. *

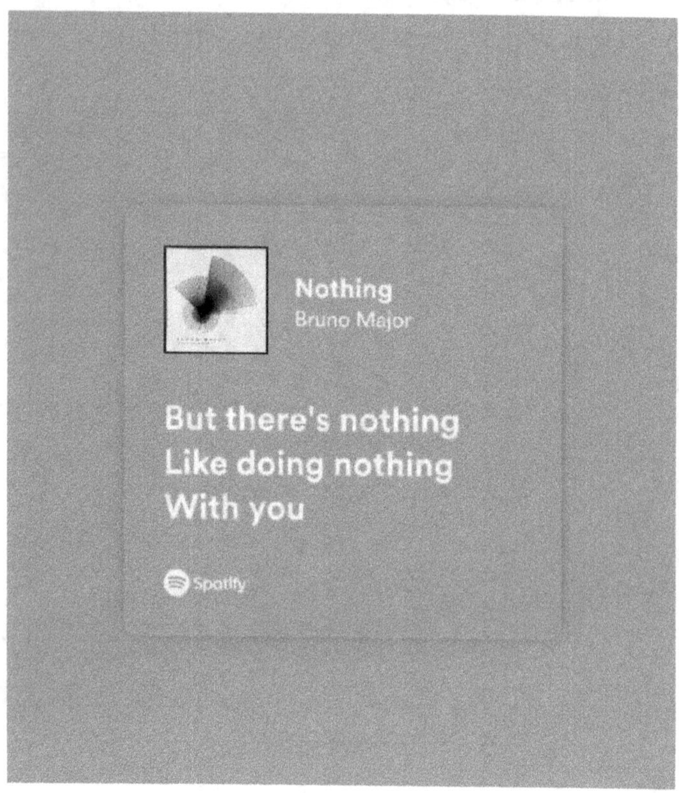

Nothing
Bruno Major

But there's nothing
Like doing nothing
With you

Spotify

17. *

Dolce far niente

The sweetness of doing nothing with you over powers doing even the craziest things with someone else. So much so, that I'd prefer sitting by you, in the cold winter morning, getting incredibly bored and sleepy, than the concert of my most recent celebrity crush.

That the thought of holding your hand, would weigh over a thousand kisses from anybody else. That knowing what you ate for lunch seems more interesting than all the gossip about the girl I hate. That remembering that you don't like eating onions appears more important than remembering all the drugs I'm supposed to.

That lighting the last cigarette of the day with you, subtles down the grandest euphoria I've had. That writing love letters for you, which I won't ever send, are worth more to me than those entire books I've written.

That having a few moments of peace with you, are apparently more than sufficient for me to function. That even when I'm just your option, feels better than being someone's first priority.

18. *

But what if,
I am the painting at the store'
Which everyone cares about enough to admire,
But not enough to bring home?

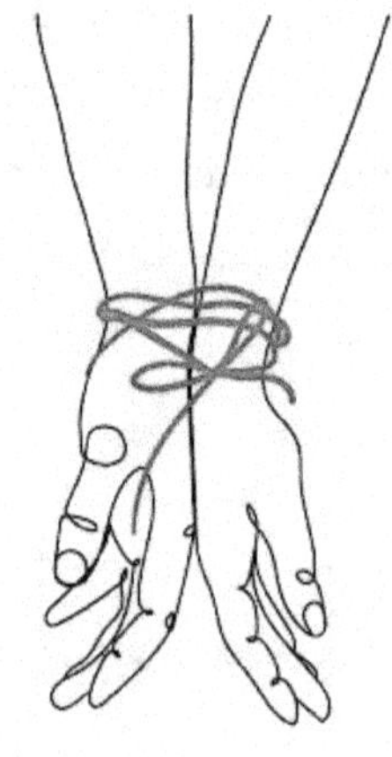

19. STAGE IV

~~DEPRESSION~~

20. *

serendipityredefined

I keep seeing flashes of the future, I never got
a chance to have with you.

21. *

In and out, out and about,
That's what it was.
One hand I'd hoe around,
And hop into pubs and bars.
I'd go out with 7 guys a month,
And blew out blunts and cigars.
Shouting profanities like shooting guns,
Walking under an unbothered facade.
Other, I'd cry myself to sleep,
Wishing, had you seen,
What was among the weeps,
What all was under the sheen.
I'd lie down, all loony,
And spend the whole day,
In bed with emo movies,
Emo songs, and other cliché.
And no matter how far I try
To run away from heartache,
There it is, in corners and cries,
Showing up, my worst mistake.
Guess, I'll just keep it down,
Won't throw up at thought,
Of guys in my town,

Or maybe, I won't,
I'd go back in a count,
To again being a hoe.

22. *

My mom told me once, "Those who are meant to be, eventually end up with one another. Not just in this life, but for lives to come and they've ended up with each other for the lives they already had. Even the squirrels you see, or the two beautiful sparrows clinging to each other you saw in the morning, have ended up together in their earlier lives and are gonna end up for next ones. So if it's meant to be, then you'd end up together. "

That's the only thing that my mom said and made sense to me. The bright side to this is that I know I wouldn't look for you in next life. We weren't meant to be, and we're not going to be. Although, out of all the disappointments and heartbreaks, the only question I'm gonna ask Him, is why didn't you end up with me. I don't even need an answer, I just want Him to know that, this was the heartbreak of the century for me. Even if I had to sacrifice the one question I had, to ask Him.

We're never meant to be. And you already knew that. Guess one of us isn't scared enough to accept that. I'd say, see you in next life, but honestly I don't want to. I wanted you in this life and this life only. I wanted it to be you and you wanted it to be someone else. I'll make sure I forget about you till the end of this life.

But what my mom didn't tell me was, what if I end up alone? Would I end up alone in next lives too? Was I always alone in previous lives too? Did He really not get someone for me? Was He out of people or did He not think I was also worthy of someone I love? So many questions to ask him, but both of us know what am I gonna ask.

....

23. *

You know what? You're a literal exception to every rule I set up, for falling in love with someone. It's as if I've been meticulously trying not to fall for you, because well, like we both know, it'd end up being an epic disaster.

Let's see what I had planned. And you know that you're the total opposite to whatever I planned. I've always fallen for guys who are hot. There's a reason behind it. With hot guys, I somewhat know that they're gonna break my heart, and since I saw it coming, I'd be prepared for it. But you. You, my dear, are a fucking human dandelion. You're so beautiful that I can't even try to describe. And that beauty caught me off guard.

I've always wanted to be with someone with different profession. Because of the clash of opinions, fights and submitting to the arguments. But I fell for you. I can't even imagine why I did that.

I wanted to fall in love with someone with as little empathy as me. I didn't want him to feel all the pain and hatred there is, in the world. And then you happened. You fucking feel everything. Why can't you feel like I feel for you?

I wanted to end up with someone with a similar or even better sense of humour than me. Someone, who's kinda satisfied with what life offered them. Someone, who cares, just a bit about what would make the other person feel appreciated.

The thing is, honey, I wanted someone who would go lengths to make someone feel good about themselves, appreciate their mere existence. You wouldn't. I wanted someone who could be relied upon. Someone who would be there even if you needed them at fucking 3 in the morning. Someone, who I can rely on. I can't, on you.

So, there are more than one reason, why I tried so damn hard, not to fall in love with you. But we both know, how that went. Honey, I'm going to distance myself from you, and kinda everybody else. I need to. I can't take the heartbreak anymore. I can't take the anxiety of you being with someone else. I can't take it. This is my breaking point. I can't. I just can't.

24. STAGE V

~~ACCEPTANCE~~

25. *

Enter Caption

26. *

"I'm hurt. No, hold on. It's more like I'm tired."
"I can totally understand."
"No, you can't. And I wish on my life, that you don't. Ever."
oooooo

"There's no end to the pain."
"Well, it's there to make you look for escapes."
"Is there an escape?"
"No. But there's an illusion that there is. And that continuous run for the escape, keeps you going."
oooooo

"I'm all caught up inside, and I can't find a way."
"And?"
"And?"
"There's more. There's always more."
"Yeah. I don't wanna think. Because when I think too much about it, I can't breathe."
oooooo

"I feel as if someone's twisting a dagger inside of me, even though, it's been a while since I've felt hurt."
"It will get better. It's all gonna be just fine in the end. Eventually."
"What if it doesn't get better? What if it doesn't get fine?"
"Then it won't matter. Because it'll be the end."

ooooo

"Because there are things that you can't talk about. They're meant to be buried in the places unreachable even to you. Where even your own silence can't really reach."
"Oh, you'd be surprised, silence is louder than you could ever imagine."
"Well, well, well. As a child, mostly I spoke inside my head. So yeah, been there, done that."

ooooo

"All my life, I tried to fill an abyss of emptiness by something that doesn't really exist. And now when that curtain is lifted, theres a whole sea of darkness staring right back at me."
"Stop staring at it then. Close your eyes. Shut it off."
"For how much longer?"

27.*

They say, "You should love people where they are. Not before that, neither after."
I tell them that I loved you where you were, and then I walked away a hundred steps, to love you from afar. Apparently I was better at loving you from a distance.

-Shruti

28. *

One day you'd find someone you can't give up on, but you have to, and you'd know what it is like to be so helpless, that all you can do is to watch them slip away. And they always slip away, the only difference being that with people who we want the least damage done due to, take the longest. I'd like you to slip away like a freaking knife, and you are slipping like fucking sand. Leaving your pieces for me to remember, and honestly I don't want it.

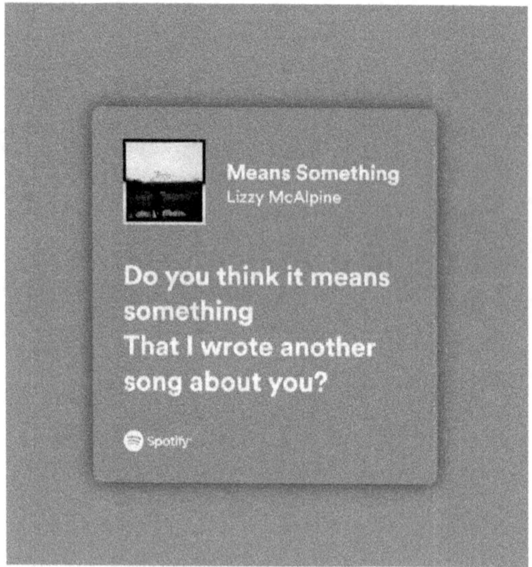

29. *

serendipityredefined

We'll survive, you and I. Separately. We can't
do it together.

~*~

"What do you want for your birthday?", I ask you, just to make sure that I don't gift you something that would overshadow the gifts given by your girlfriend.

I don't know what got me to ask you that, it's not like I could ever replace her.

You tell me that you don't want anything. I say okay.

**

Your birthday is 3 weeks away, and I wrote you a book. Hopefully it would get to you in time.

www.ingramcontent.com/pod-product-compliance
Lightning Source LLC
Chambersburg PA
CBHW070607160726
48003CB00005B/2152